One Christmas in
Old Tascosa

One Christmas in Old Tascosa

CASANDRA FIRMAN

As Told by
Quintille Speck-Firman Garmany

Foreword by Red Steagall

ILLUSTRATED BY JUDY WISE

Texas Tech University Press

The paper used in this book meets the minimum requirements of
ANSI/NISO Z39.48-1992 (R1997). ∞

Library of Congress Cataloging-in-Publication Data
Firman, Casandra.
   One Christmas in Old Tascosa / Casandra Firman ; as told by
Quintille Speck-Firman Garmany ; foreword by Red Steagall.
      p.   cm.
   Summary: "Illustrated Christmas memoir. Quintille Speck-Firman
Garmany, who was seven in 1931, recalls her Christmas pageant that
year in Old Tascosa's one-room schoolhouse, how the Depression
and Dust Bowl affected her and her classmates' lives, and how an
unpredicted blizzard introduced her to Frenchie McCormick. Two
historical photographs. Song lyrics"—Provided by publisher.
   ISBN-13: 978-0-89672-588-1 (litho-case : alk. paper)
   ISBN-10: 0-89672-588-X (litho-case : alk. paper)
   1. Garmany, Quintille Speck-Firman—Childhood and youth. 2.
Tascosa (Tex.)—Biography. 3. Christmas—Texas—Tascosa—History
—20th century. 4. Depressions—1929—Texas—Tascosa. 5. Tascosa
(Tex.)—Social life and customs. 6. Old-time music—Texas.
I. Garmany, Quintille Speck-Firman. II. Title.
   F394.T17F57 2006
   976.4'063092—dc22
   [B]   2006012885

Printed in the United States of America
06 07 08 09 10 11 12 13 14 / 9 8 7 6 5 4 3 2 1
T S

Texas Tech University Press, Box 41037,
Lubbock, Texas 79409-1037 USA
800.832.4042 ttup@ttu.edu
www.ttup.ttu.edu

*To the children of Tascosa, past
and present*

CONTENTS

YOUNGSTERS on the Texas Plains today would have a hard time fathoming the devastation and poverty brought on by the Great Depression and the Dust Bowl. Like the first settlers who migrated to the Great Plains, people who lived off the land had only one priority: survival. When the Depression brought soup lines to the cities, many farmers and ranchers managed to survive by growing their own food. Then the drought and the Dust Bowl came. No crops would grow. Farmers and ranchers had to look to other places for work while their lands sat idle. It fell to their wives to keep the children safe, fed, and clothed the best way they knew how, using only those resources at hand. In cities and in the country alike, folks found themselves in the same basket: hungry and desperate.

In every concrete detail, Quintille's story, so poignantly retold by her daughter Casandra, speaks volumes about the human condition on the High Plains in 1931. It is hard to imagine that anything so simple as a lead pencil could break a budget or that two in one school year could constitute extravagance. Yet children in Old Tascosa at the end of the Depression and on the cusp of even more desperate times were, like their counterparts elsewhere on the Plains, accustomed to hardship and well-accustomed to shouldering their share of the family's burden. They had no reason to know that life could be different or had any way of knowing what constituted luxury. Not knowing that they were deprived, they found joy in friendships and games, and in the wonders of the schoolroom, as children will. And in the simplest of Christmas pageants they found the prospect of bliss.

Having grown up in the Texas Panhandle as the product of Depression-era parents, I can empathize with Quintille and her classmates. In the late forties and early fifties, many families still struggled financially, even though most everyone had a job. The fifties would bring a new affluence to the nation at large, but the Plains were still in recovery. The Panhandle weather didn't help matters. I vividly recall dust storms when you couldn't see twelve inches in front of you. I can still feel the blizzards that left drifts twenty feet high.

Elizabeth "Frenchie" McCormick was already a legend in Tascosa by the time this story takes place. Her fame as a dance hall girl and her devotion to her husband Mickey, a gambler and livery stable owner, have been the subject of fable and lore, drama, and song. Yet what is unquestionable is how her love for Mickey kept Frenchie in a dying town twenty-seven years after his death. Mickey died in 1912; Tascosa in 1916. From then until the county forced her to leave in 1939, Frenchie led a lonely and meager existence as the town's only resident.

Yet little Quintille Speck, only seven when this story takes place, was one of a dozen rural children still attending the Old Tascosa schoolhouse in 1931. The confluences of forces that bring their Christmas pageant to unfold at this pivotal moment in history, poised between wind and winter, deprivation and despair, at the far edge of an era that defined the Western frontier, deserve our attention and our wonder.

I suppose this story touches me so because it is set in a place that I know and love. Remembering the sacrifices that my mother made raising six wild kids on a schoolteacher's salary, I identify with the people of Old Tascosa and with their struggles. Because my lifelong fondness for the Panhandle evolved long ago into a penchant for its history, I may have a little more insight into the place and the people that Quintille knew. But I believe with all my heart that readers everywhere will be deeply affected and enriched by the struggle, sacrifice, and spirit that make this one of the most transcendent and moving stories I have ever encountered. Read and enjoy.

RED STEAGALL
2006

One Christmas in
Old Tascosa

November 2004—A Prologue

MY MOTHER'S HANDS patted out biscuits as she looked through my kitchen window. At eighty-one, the process was so familiar she didn't have to think about what came next. "Looks like snow," she said. I followed her gaze. From my Pacific Northwest kitchen, I could see Puget Sound. An early morning ferry was making its passage to Seattle. The water reflected the dark gray clouds overhead; but no, it wasn't going to snow that day.

"Looks like it, but my guess is more rain," my sister responded, not looking up from the apples she was slicing. As I watched them work, I wondered how many more Thanksgivings we would have together.

"But snow is unpredictable." Mother paused and gazed through the window; the view of the ferry was obscured by a cedar tree and was nearly out of sight. "I remember a storm . . . in Texas . . . in Tascosa. I was a little girl." She sighed and shook her head. "I haven't thought about it for years. It was a snowstorm." Something in her voice stopped my sister and me. Susan put down her paring knife and I leaned against the counter.

"Tell us," Susan asked, and our mother began a story so fascinating that, after hearing it, we were determined to take her back to the Texas Panhandle. We wanted to jog her memories and for her to tell us more.

We made the trip in May 2005. Mother flew in from Florida, Susan from Arizona, and I from Washington. Mother recounted the story again, sometimes adding or changing names, places, and order of happenings as the landscape sparked memories of the Great Depression on the Texas Plains.

We traveled in a rental car over the land of her childhood and stayed up late in our hotel room drinking coffee and eating the free cookies offered up at the front desk. My mother's telling grew richer as time and place returned, commanding the past to rise and stand before her with the added benefit of wisdom and meaning wrought by the passage of time. This is the story she told us.

I

Tascosa, 1931

I AM OFTEN surprised to find that some
people think it doesn't snow in Texas. Well, it
does. In Old Tascosa, the winters could be as
cold and fierce as the summers were hot. Tascosa,
a small town in the Texas Panhandle, a town that
no longer exists, was my home a very long time
ago.

In 1931, the last year my family lived there, Tascosa was little more than a few farms scattered
over flat stretches of land broken up here and
there with sagebrush-covered hills and cottonwood.

A casual passerby might have glanced at the
surrounding countryside and called it barren, but
it wasn't. In the spring, the meandering creek beds
became ribbons of green grass polka-dotted with
wildflowers. In summer, the ribbons turned the
color of butterscotch and were home to my pets—
the grasshoppers, snakes, and beetles I captured,
brought home, and then released after my mother
discovered them. My sisters and I, three girls in

ragged dungarees with long unkempt hair, ran barefoot through the creek beds and over the rolling hills. In complete defiance of our father's warnings, we teased rattlesnakes with sticks. We picked flowers in the spring and in the summer played hide and seek in the cottonwoods and in the tall, dry grass covering the prairie. With twigs and mud we fashioned little houses for dolls we didn't have, and made mud cakes, decorating them carefully with buttercups and wishing they were real. We pressed our feet into the mud and felt its soft, doughy texture ooze between our toes. Above us and all around us, meadowlarks called out to one another, their music more beautiful than any I have ever heard.

Looking back, I realize that the dwelling we called home was hardly more than a shack. It was made of adobe bricks and had two rooms other than the kitchen. My sisters and I slept in a single bed in one room, my parents and baby brother in the other. The ceiling was low, and the roof was so patched that had it ever rained while I lived there, the water would have flowed through the roof like a sprinkler. When the wind blew, it hissed through cracks in the walls, stirring up dust in the summer and inviting the bitter cold in winter. It sounds grim, I suppose, but I didn't know of any other way to live. As far as I could tell, most of our neighbors lived pretty much the same.

My mother grew vegetables in a garden next to our house. Sometimes, when money was scarce,

Her garden supplied the only food we had.

her garden supplied the only food we had. In those days, and in that place, money was always scarce, and people were often hungry. During my few years in Tascosa, I watched as the fields, once rich with corn and wheat, grew dry. When the earth could no longer sustain it, the grass that had blanketed the plains gave way to sagebrush. We looked for rain, we prayed for rain, but rain didn't come. Soon, the dry, cracked land would become dust.

People all over the country were without jobs, without food, and without homes. Men wandered from farm to farm asking for work, and, if there was no work, they asked if they could chop some wood or mend a fence or do anything for a meal. For a time, a day didn't pass without a man coming to our door and asking for food. They wouldn't accept the food without working for it, and mother always gave them something to eat, even when we had almost nothing ourselves. I cherish the memory of my mother's kindness toward those men. You see, her heart had grown dry and unyielding, hand-in-hand with the earth; I want to remember her fondly, to match my memories of Old Tascosa, my childhood home.

2

Tascosa, 1880

BEFORE I LIVED THERE; before I was born, Old Tascosa was a booming town. In 1880 it had everything that a cowboy town in the old West ought to have—saloons, gambling rooms, and its full share of outlaws.

Billy the Kid spent some time there. So did a famous lawman named Pat Garret. As a matter of fact, Pat Garret shot and killed Billy, but that's another story. There were plenty of gunfights in those days—gunfights between ranchers and farmers, sheriffs and outlaws, cowboys and other cowboys, and outlaws and other outlaws. The men on the losing side of those gunfights ended up on Boot Hill, a lonely cemetery just outside of town.

Where there are outlaws, cowboys, and gunfights, there are saloons and dance hall girls. Old Tascosa had them all, and of all the dance hall girls, one stood out from the rest. Her name was Frenchie McCormick.

No one knew exactly where she came from, and for a time, nobody knew her real name. The fact that she was born in Louisiana and danced on the burlesque stages of New Orleans has been well-established, but her life before the dance halls was, and still is to this day, speculation. Who was she? Was she a girl running away from a tyrannical father? Was she bolting from the convent school her wealthy family insisted she attend? Perhaps she had a past to escape, or maybe, she simply wanted adventure and thought she might find it in the Wild West. Whatever life she left behind, and for reasons she kept to herself, Frenchie left the glamour and relative sophistication of New Orleans sometime before 1880 and made her way to Mobeetie, a wild Texas town in the vicinity of Fort Elliot.

She was soon dancing in a Mobeetie saloon, charming the resident soldiers, buffalo hunters, and cowboys who patronized it. Dark curls framed her lovely face, and her satin gowns sparkled almost as brightly as her deep blue eyes. She mesmerized her audience as she swirled and dipped, skirts floating just high enough to reveal white, lacy petticoats, pantaloons, and slender ankles. Perhaps Mickey first saw Frenchie as she danced.

Mickey McCormick was a livery stable owner, but better known in Tascosa as a gambler. Where they met is a fact—in the Mobeetie Saloon—but I'm not sure exactly *how* they met. I like to think that as he sauntered through the saloon on his way to the gaming tables, he looked toward the stage and caught a glimpse of lace swaying beneath a

Dark curls framed her lovely face . . .

skirt of crimson satin. Raising his head, he saw her face, glowing and flushed and her eyes sparkling like sapphires. By chance, she glanced down. She fixed her eyes on him, and they found themselves locked in a gaze. Maybe he stood at the foot of the stage and watched her, forgetting the card games in the back room; maybe, after she had danced, he took flowers to her dressing room.

This, of course, is speculation. I don't know the particulars of their first meeting. What I do know is that Frenchie fell in love with Mickey, and Mickey fell in love with Frenchie. He brought her to his home, an adobe shack next to his livery stable, and in Old Tascosa, they made a life together.

People fall in love all the time, but not all love is created equal. Frenchie and Mickey's love was the kind of love that we all hope to find, but not all of us are so lucky. They breathed only because it allowed them one more day to be together. The passion and intensity of their love lasted through each day of the thirty-two years of their marriage. It endured as Frenchie's youthful beauty faded and as her round cheeks sunk into her face and collapsed into wrinkles. It endured long after she traded her satin gowns and her petticoats for simple cotton dresses in shades of gray and black. Their love endured after the railroad bypassed Tascosa, after the ranchers and cowboys moved on to better ranges, and after the saloons and gambling halls closed. Frenchie's love for Mickey

endured even after his death in 1912. She continued to love him, and she continued to be true
to him. She had promised Mickey never to leave
Tascosa, and she meant to keep that pledge.

The town crumbled into dust around her—the
saloons, the livery stables, the stores, and the
homes slowly faded as neglect, abandonment, and
the forces of nature took them to the ground. All
that remained was the courthouse, the single-
room church that also served as the school, and
Frenchie and Mickey's home. For twenty-seven
years she lived alone in the ghost town that was
once Tascosa. Looking out from her door, Frenchie
could see the hilltop where her beloved Mickey lay
buried. She intended to remain close to him, and
she intended to remain in Tascosa, a town she
believed would one day be reborn in its former
glory.

In 1931, with the saloons long closed and the
cowboys gone, Tascosa was little more than a
memory. As a child in one of the few families
remaining in the countryside around the old town,
I played within the sight of Boot Hill. I heard all
the old tales about the outlaws and the gamblers
and, of course, about Frenchie McCormick. And in
that year, I was lucky enough to meet her.

3

The Morning of the Pageant
Tascosa, December 16, 1931

I N   S O M E   W A Y S , the day of the Christmas pageant began like any other. Every morning I'd wake and laze in bed daydreaming until I heard my mother moving about in the kitchen. I'd hear her starting a fire in the cook stove and putting the kettle on to boil. Usually, my father would have already left by the time I awoke, but sometimes I'd hear him saying good-bye to Mother and the sound of the slamming door behind him. When I could smell the coffee, I'd hop out of bed and dress for school, and by the time my mother was shouting, "Girls, get up. Get up now. Do you hear me? You'll be late," I was dressed. Then I'd go into the kitchen and help my mother stir the oatmeal. That's the way it was every morning, and that's the way it was the morning of the pageant.

On other days, my sisters Roma and Jane would stay in bed until the last possible moment, rising and dressing only after mother threatened them with a whipping, a whipping that they knew she would deliver. Then they would throw on whatever clothes they had been wearing the day before and scramble into the kitchen. Mother would put spoonfuls of oatmeal into our bowls, all the while enumerating our faults and shortcomings. "You girls are the laziest girls I know. Don't know how I raised such lazy girls. Straighten your shoulders, Quintille."

But the morning of the pageant was different. Jane and Roma kept pace with me, all *three* of us had sprung from bed when the scent of coffee first entered our room. Jane pulled on her dungarees, and on any other day so would Roma and I, but that morning, we put on dresses. They hung on us like flour sacks, but neither of us knew the difference. Like most of the other girls, we wore pants to school and had little need for dresses. Because we had only one dress each, it was a lucky thing that we thought they were pretty. Mine was a grayish-blue plaid; Roma's a rusty color with faint white stripes. They each had round white colors and turned-up white cuffs. The collar and cuffs made them especially pretty, but mainly they were pretty because they had sashes that we tied in the back. Although we dressed hurriedly that morning, we made sure that we tied one another's sashes in big, perfect bows.

Our thick hair had been braided just the day before, and we saw no reason to unbraid it simply to comb it out and braid again. But because this was a special day, we spit on our hands and pasted the stray hairs into place. Our dressing was complete when we pulled on thick woolen socks and the lace-up boots Mother and Father had splurged on that autumn. "You look nice," Roma said, "do I look nice?"

"You look very nice, very pretty and very nice," I answered.

We burst into the kitchen just as Mother was turning from the stove and preparing to shout her first wake-up call. She saw us, took in a breath and said, "You're up." She paused, opened her mouth as if to speak, then closed it. I believe she was so surprised that she could think of nothing to say. Just then, behind her on the kitchen table, my sisters and I saw something that left us equally speechless.

Mother made biscuits a few times each week, and those biscuits were our mainstay. They substituted for bread, and they filled our empty stomachs when the meat and vegetables were depleted. When we were lucky, we had butter to go with them, occasionally we had peanut butter, and, on rare and special occasions, Mother would bring out the wild plum jam. On that morning, the morning of the pageant, sitting on the kitchen table was an empty jar, and next to it, a tin plate covered with biscuits. Each biscuit was split down the center, and then rejoined with a layer of wild plum jam. Mother had arranged them in a circular pattern that rose, pyramid-like, and terminated in a single biscuit with a dollop of jam on its top. It was beautiful.

"Keep your hands off those," Mother said when she noticed us gazing at the plate of biscuits with poorly concealed longing, "I'm taking them to the pageant."

Roma and I exchanged glances.

"It's a party, isn't it? Civilized people serve this sort of thing at parties." She turned to the stove and gave the oatmeal a final stir.

Jane, standing eye-level with the table, inspected the jam sandwiches in amazement. The smell was almost too tempting to resist, and I half expected her to reach out and snatch one when she thought Mother wasn't watching. Somehow, Mother was thinking the same thing. "Keep your hands off those, Jane," she snapped, and Jane backed away. I often wondered how Mother could read our minds. She was aware of every misdeed we committed—and even those we were only considering.

"But, I get to go to the party. I get to eat party cakes, don't I, Mama?" Jane asked with a pleading whimper.

"Not if you keep up that pouting." Jane looked away and said nothing.

Mother turned to Roma and me. "Your father will be coming. Mr. Turner's going to the gravel pit to get him and the others. Then he'll swing 'round and fetch me and Jane and the baby." She stopped to remove her apron and place it on a nail. "We'll all be there. Everyone in these parts will be there, I believe. I'm expecting you to do well. Hear? Don't

The smell was almost too tempting to resist . . .

be forgetting your lines. Stay on tune. I want folks to know I raised you right. Make me and your dad proud."

Roma and I were silent, but we were on alert. There was nothing we wanted more than to make our mother proud. We had no doubt that our father was proud of us, but our mother's regard always seemed just beyond our reach. We believed we could earn it that day. We *would* make her proud. Roma and I had practiced. We knew not to turn our backs to the audience. We knew how to curtsy holding out our skirts like a tent and bending one knee. We knew our lines so well we could repeat them in our sleep. I could sing my solo in a clear, loud voice, enunciating every consonant, every vowel, so that there was no mistaking my words. "Up on the rooftop, click, click, click, down from the chimney comes good St. Nick. Ho, ho, ho, who wouldn't know. . . ."

Roma and I finished breakfast and wrapped ourselves in the short wool coats our mother had made from one of hers. "Off you go," she said. "I won't have you late." We stepped outside and turned to wave. Mother nodded in our direction before she closed the door. I thought she smiled, but I could have been wrong. We stood and waited for Mr. Turner to pull up in his touring Desoto.

Mr. Turner's car was the only one for miles around that was large enough to carry the five children who rode in it. We called it our school bus. Jane, too young for school, waited with us, tormenting us the way only a five-year-old can—pulling our hair, running circles around us, and taunting, "You can't catch me, you can't catch me," when of course, nobody wanted to catch her.

Today would be the best day of our lives. We knew it, had longed and prepared for it, and now it was here. Everyone was coming—all of our parents were going to be there. On top of that, our teacher, Mrs. Talley, had invited each living soul within a five-mile radius. If they all showed up (and most said they would), there would be at least twenty-three people there to watch us sing, read poems, and act in a play. I was giddy with anticipation.

I imagined the array of cakes, candies, and popcorn balls that mothers of twelve students could produce—twelve students from six families and six plates covered with food. Of course, Mrs. Talley would bring something, making seven plates covered in treats. "Roma," I said as Mr. Turner pulled in, "if every mom makes a treat like our mom did, there'll be enough sweets to fill a candy store. I'm going to eat and eat and eat."

Roma giggled. "Umm, umm." She said, "I'm gonna eat 'til I burst."

"I'll burst before you do," I squealed. Laughing, we climbed into our bus and greeted its occupants, all wearing their best clothes and grinning as wide as their faces would permit. They didn't know why we were giggling, but they joined in. Even Mr. Turner began to laugh. *This day would be like no other. I knew it.*

We looked out the window to wave to Jane, but we saw that she had already run into the house. The cold did not permit her to stay. It was deathly cold that morning—and dark. Clouds, gray and heavy, sagged in the sky.

4

Our School Day Begins

E WERE THE LAST students to arrive at school. As we pulled into the yard, Robert and his sister, Polly, were unhitching their horse from its wagon and about to tie him under a shelter next to Chester, an elderly sway-backed farm horse who shuttled George to and from school each day. George and the Balfour boys, P. H., Jimmy, and Bill, were playing "Annie over," a game in which one team threw a ball over the roof of the school, the other team retrieved it, and then propelled it back over the roof again. The object of the game and its exact rules are lost to me now, but I do remember that each time they tossed the ball they'd shout "Annie over."

I wondered why the Balfour boys were at school so early. They walked to school each day and normally timed their arrival to coincide with the school bell's first ring. I stood back and watched them play. I was in awe of the Balfour boys. Gangly and disheveled as they were, they were like royalty to me. Their father owned land, and they lived in a real house; that is, a house made of wood instead of adobe bricks, a house with a parlor and a fireplace. The Balfours were royalty, and Jimmy, the one closest to me in age, was a prince. Never mind that he made fun of my red hair. Never mind that he called me "freckle speck." I loved Jimmy Balfour.

That day I felt bold. Without stopping to think I shouted, "How'd you get here so early, Jimmy?"

"Ran."

"You ran four miles?"

"Yep."

"It was too cold to walk," George hollered, "so they had to run. Annie over," and George hurled the ball over the one-story frame building. Jimmy ran to the other side of the school to try and catch it.

The children with caps pulled them down to cover their ears. Those without caps hunched their shoulders, trying to keep their ears close to their collars. The children without mittens wore socks on their hands or kept them in their pockets. Only George was bare handed. Occasionally he cupped his hands over his mouth and warmed them with his breath, but other than that, he behaved as if the cold meant nothing to him. Mary, one of the girls who rode the bus with Roma and me, huddled with Polly in the school yard whispering, the two of them glancing now and then at George, and squealing with glee each time he tossed the ball.

"The big girls," I thought, "they always act so silly when George is around." I couldn't understand why they were stuck on George. He was such a show-off. He always had to be the fastest, the strongest, and the cleverest. That wasn't much of a feat for a kid who was older than everyone else. He was thirteen, nearly fourteen. Now Jimmy, he was a gentleman, a prince. I only wished that he'd notice me other than when he wanted someone to tease.

Just the week before, I had tried to get his attention by snatching his lunch sack and dropping it into the outhouse. It worked, and he chased me around the yard a few times and then seemed to lose interest. I told him I was sorry and gave him my lunch. I hoped that he would sit with me and eat it, but he didn't. He ran over to where the other boys were and ate with them. I finished the day hungry and a bit embarrassed.

But today was different. Today he spoke to me; maybe it was just two words, but it was a start. I hummed to myself as I skipped all the way to the school's door. I arrived just as Mrs. Talley was opening it. She was holding a brass bell by its wooden handle. "Good Morning, Quintille," she said, "don't you look pretty today."

I thought Mrs. Talley looked pretty, too, although I didn't tell her that. I remember Mrs. Talley as a big woman, but in retrospect, she probably wasn't much more than average size. She pulled her hair up into a bun and kept it in place with little combs covered in rhinestones. She had only two or three dresses, and they were simple, but every day she wore a white apron with blue cornflowers embroidered across the hem and on the pockets. She kept a pencil in one pocket and a pair of scissors and a handkerchief in the other. The combs in Mrs. Talley's hair intrigued me, as did the embroidered cornflowers on her apron. But what charmed me—and made her so pretty— was her smile. When Mrs. Talley smiled, the clouds parted. There wasn't a student that didn't love her and there wasn't a student who didn't believe that Mrs. Talley loved them back. She was that kind of woman.

Mrs. Talley rang the bell. Everyone stopped what they were doing and looked in her direction. We waited for the signal that would tell us the school day had begun.

"All right class," shouted Mrs. Talley, "up the hill with you—last one back's a rotten apple."

Like rabbits before hounds we raced up the hill. I may have started further away than the others, but I was fast and knew I could make up the time I'd lost. Shouting, "Here I come," I darted after my friends. I passed Roma, a year older than me, but skinnier and slow. I passed Mary and Polly, who tried to be dainty and purposefully slow when they ran. I passed all of the others until only George, Jimmy, P.H., and Helen, a nine-year-old, remained in front.

The cold was forgotten as I scampered over the

Shouting, "Here I come," I darted after my friends.

rocks and gopher holes, screaming and laughing. By the time I reached the school, I was tied with Helen for fourth place. George, of course, was first and P.H. second. Jimmy, in third place, looked in my direction as he tried to catch his breath. "Not bad for a girl," he said. My heart leapt, although I wasn't sure if he was directing his words to me or Helen.

The race up the hill and back was the way we started every school day, and we thought it was grand. When the race ended, we met at the door, and Mrs. Talley ushered us into school. Our school was just one room furnished with a piano, a pot-bellied stove, and enough chairs and desks for twelve students. Despite the vigorous race we had just completed, we were cold; it was reassuring to find the stove lit and most of the chill gone from the room. Once through the door, we gathered at the piano. It was time for our second ritual of the day.

"Caught your breath, children?" asked Mrs. Talley, and without waiting for our answer, she commenced to pound out a tune. That morning it was "The Red River Valley." With the same zeal we used to run up the hill, we sang about the Red River. It was my favorite song, and that day, Mrs. Talley ended it by playing the chorus twice. I was happy! Everyone was happy!

5

Mrs. Talley Plans Our Day

THE SONG ENDED; we remained standing next to the piano. "Boys and girls," Mrs. Talley said, "it's time for lessons."

A frozen silence followed her announcement, broken by an outburst from a distraught Mary. "But, Mrs. Talley—the pageant," she called out, "today's the pageant and we aren't . . ."

Mrs. Talley interrupted, "Mary, I think you forgot to raise your hand."

Mary raised her hand.

"Yes, Mary."

Mary took in a deep breath and a cascade of words tumbled from her mouth. "The room's not decorated, and some of us haven't finished our paper chains, and we need to get the tree decorated, too, but first we have to get a tree, and we don't even have a tree so we won't have time for lessons." She took a breath, "and besides, some of us just need some time to freshen up and maybe comb our hair. We just don't have time for lessons."

The class stood perfectly still, scanning Mrs. Talley's face for a sign that she would give in. None of us imagined that we would have schoolwork that day. Mrs. Talley was perpetually cheerful, yet perpetually resolved. Her word was law in our classroom, but her laws were easy to obey. Today, if she didn't relent, it might not be so easy.

"Well," she said with a serious and thoughtful look about her, "I think that we need to exercise our brains; after all, next week's a vacation week. Your brains will turn to mush if we don't fill them with arithmetic, reading, and history." We received her words in silence and then turned and dragged ourselves to our desks.

"Hmm," we heard Mrs. Talley say. Those of us who had not already slumped into our seats stopped to listen. "Mary does have a point about those crepe paper chains." We turned, hopefully, and faced our teacher. The students sitting at their desks raised their heads.

"How does this sound? Why don't we work until lunch time, and then, no more lessons for the rest of the day? We'll have a full two and a half hours to decorate and practice the pageant and sing a few songs—what do you say? It will be like one big party before the real party!"

The younger children let out a cheer as if they'd just been given the entire day off. The older ones looked at one another perplexed, confused as to whether they had won the argument or lost it. Mrs. Talley smiled.

Mary took in a deep breath. . . . "The room's not decorated . . ."

6

The Pencil

THE FIRST SUBJECT after our morning song was always reading, and it took us up to eleven o'clock. I was not much of a reader at that time, although I later became a voracious consumer of books. I don't recall what I read that day, but know that one of the big kids read with me. The big kids were assigned to the younger ones as tutors.

Arithmetic followed reading and it lasted until noon. Mrs. Talley taught the younger children, and George, P.H., and Polly divided the rest of the students among themselves and became our teachers. Who taught them, I'll never know; but they knew more than we did, and the system seemed to work.

Even though they were nine and I was only seven, I sat with Jimmy and Helen for arithmetic. I was good at numbers and held my own with the nine-year-olds. When the weather was good, we'd go outside and have contests answering multiplication problems. Each correct answer was a point.

We usually tied, but Polly would say that I was the real winner because I was younger than the others. That embarrassed me. One, I didn't like Helen's feelings to be hurt; and two, I didn't want Jimmy to be reminded that I was only seven.

Helen was my friend. I didn't like to compete with her. I wanted her to win as often as I did, and I wanted her to be happy. Although she was plain and wore the same dull ribbon in her hair every day, I told her she looked pretty and that her ribbon made her look even prettier. Whenever she combed her hair a different way, I complimented it. She flattered me in the same way, and the two of us were comfortable with each other's acceptance and never questioned its sincerity. Only one aspect of our friendship caused me worry, and that was the mounting evidence that Jimmy might like her more than me. If that were the case, I might be inclined to tell her that her ribbon wasn't pretty after all, and her hair looked like moldy straw.

The morning droned on. We had started long division the week before, and Polly decided she would test us on exactly how much we had learned. She had made flash cards and held them up, one at a time, while we wrote the answers on the back of the paper we had used the day before. Helen bent over her desk, her arms forming a barricade around her work. Despite her attempts at concealment, I saw her fingers dragging across the paper as she wrote; her pencil was hardly long enough to hold. I thought it was mean of Polly to have us write the answers. We could have just as easily called out the answers the way we did in our multiplication contests. Polly knew that Helen's pencil was little more than a stub. It was plain to see that if sharpened it would be reduced to nothing more than shavings.

The year before, Helen's parents gave her two pencils. By May, both were worn to the point of total uselessness. With poorly concealed humiliation, she borrowed from her classmates to get through until the school year ended. That summer, her father left to find work. As far as I know, he never came home again. Her mother sold eggs to make money, but as the drought worsened, the chickens laid fewer and fewer eggs. When the new school year began, Helen's mother could give her only one pencil. By December, it was nearly gone. She wrote with the lightest touch, trying to conserve what lead remained. The result was writing so faint it could scarcely be read, and a little girl humiliated by such a concrete proof of her poverty.

Watching Helen, my own new pencil in hand, I was ashamed. My thoughts were mean and driven by envy—I knew they were wrong. But still, I didn't want Jimmy to like her.

Polly was not particularly interested in the lesson. She would hold up a card, then look wistfully around the room, seeming to forget what she was doing. We would finish one problem and then wait patiently for the next. Between problems, I sang Christmas carols in my head. Jimmy was fiddling around with something in his desk. Helen seemed to be using the time to daydream. Maybe she was singing carols silently, too. Maybe she was thinking about her father.

Polly was holding a card, waiting for us to finish the problem when I noticed Jimmy trying to get Helen's attention. "Psst, Helen," he whispered. Helen looked at him, shook her head rapidly, and turned her eyes back to her work.

I would have been surprised that Polly didn't hear Jimmy's whispers had she not been gazing at George, who, by the way, was gazing back at her. Polly's face was crimson. So was George's. George put his thumbs in his ears and stuck out his tongue. He crossed his eyes and wiggled his fingers at Polly. A muffled chortle escaped her lips, which she disguised as a cough. Then she covered her face with the flash card and pretended to sneeze as her shoulders shook with laughter. While Polly was taking out a handkerchief to add the finishing touch to her charade, Jimmy took the opportunity to try once more to get Helen's attention. "Psst, psst," he whispered, "Helen."

Helen shot a glance at him and whispered back, "Shush, Jimmy, we'll get in trouble." She looked away again.

"Helen," Jimmy persisted.

I looked at Polly. George was walking by, apparently on his way to talk to Mrs. Talley. As he passed, he slipped a note into Polly's hand. She

"Helen, . . . I got you a Christmas present."

took it, and while holding the flash card in one hand, she opened the note with the other. Whatever was going on between Jimmy and Helen, Polly did not seem to notice. She read the note and blushed.

"Helen," Jimmy repeated, still whispering, "I got you a Christmas present."

My heart sunk. If I were to have stood up, my knees would have buckled under me. It was Helen he liked.

Helen looked up again. Her eyes darted back and forth between Polly and Jimmy, and then they settled on Jimmy. "Really?" she whispered.

"Really." Jimmy reached into his desk and brought out something wrapped in what I recognized as the crepe paper we had been using to make decorations. He passed it to Helen. She took it, placed it in front of her, and carefully removed the paper.

It was a pencil. It wasn't a new one, but it was nearly new. "Do you like it?" whispered Jimmy. But Helen didn't respond. She held the pencil in front of her. I watched her study it, turning it, and touching the lead with a finger. I couldn't tell if she was happy or embarrassed or ashamed to receive Jimmy's gift. After a careful inspection, she rewrapped the pencil in the crepe paper and clutched it in her hand. Then she bent over so that her hair curtained most of her face. Was she crying?

"Helen, do you like it?" Jimmy's voice was

louder this time, loud enough to divert Polly from the distraction of a love note.

"Jimmy, you be quiet. Quintille and Helen, don't encourage him."

I was outraged. I was about to complain that I was not the one encouraging Jimmy. Helen was, not me. I was about to say that they were keeping me from working on my division and that Polly should tell Mrs. Talley, because if Polly didn't tell then I surely would. I wanted to do whatever I could to hurt Jimmy and Helen, because they had certainly hurt me.

But before I could say anything, Mrs. Talley made the announcement. "Children, you may put your work away. Time for lunch and then . . ." she paused for dramatic effect, "time for fun!"

"Yippee!" someone shouted, and the room was abruptly filled with chatter and movement. During the chaos of the moment, Helen put the pencil into her desk. She turned to Jimmy, who had been watching her ever since he had given her the pencil. She spoke quietly, "Yes, Jimmy. I like it. Thank you."

"Good," Jimmy said, "I hoped you would," and he left to see if he could help Mrs. Talley wash the blackboard. I looked at Helen, scanning her for flaws. I thought her dress was ugly and that her hair *did* look like straw. Her ribbon was limp and faded. I wanted to tell her that—I wanted to remind her that she was so poor that she had to go around begging for a pencil. As much as I wanted to say those things, the words just wouldn't come out.

I watched Helen take the pencil back out of her desk. It was still wrapped. She opened her present again, and she wrote something that I couldn't see on a corner of the crepe paper wrapping. She looked at what she had written, and then she smiled. Helen glanced up and saw me watching her. Her smile vanished. "Quinn," she began, glancing worriedly in the direction of the other children, "don't tell where I got this pencil, please?" Still trying to think of something mean to say to her, I didn't answer.

My sister Roma walked by. "Helen, Quinn, you gonna help us sweep? We're gonna make the room real nice, so d'ya wanna hel . . ." She stopped, seeing the pencil in Helen's hand. "Where'd ya get the pencil, Helen?"

"My mama gave it to me."

"Oh, that's nice," said Roma without giving it another thought. "So, you wanna help?"

"I'll help," Helen answered, returning the pencil to her desk. Roma scampered to the back of the room where two brooms hung from nails in the wall. "Quinn," Helen said. I looked at her. "You won't tell, will you?"

"Naw, I won't tell. I'll say the same as you if anyone asks—your mama gave it to you."

"My mama wants to give me a new pencil," Helen said, "'cept right now she can't."

I paused, needing to make a decision before

speaking again. "Come on, Helen, let's help get ready." She stood and held her hand out to me. I took it. Then, hand-in-hand, the two of us skipped off to join the others

I didn't want to be mean to Helen any longer. Besides, nothing could ruin this day for me. *Today was the Christmas pageant. Today was going to be the best day of my life.*

7

The Snow

RECALLING OUR PREPARATIONS, I see a wash of color and movement. I hear the joyful sounds of children, free from worry, singing and laughing—and in the background, a piano, sounding slightly off key, but lively, cheerful, and happy.

We ran through the performance one last time, a dress rehearsal as Mrs. Talley called it, although there weren't any costumes. Then, practiced, prepared, and confident, we proceeded to make the room festive. Some of us drew pictures of Christmas trees and candy canes on the chalkboard. Jimmy and his brothers brought a mesquite tree into the room and stood it in a bucket filled with stones. Paper chains of red and green circled the tree. I have no idea where the colored paper came from. Paper was a valuable commodity, to use it purely and simply for decoration was extravagant.

George and P.H. stoked the fire, then arranged the desks in three straight rows and added a bench to accommodate our audience. The older girls covered a table with brightly colored cloths brought from home. That was where the food would go. Giggling and whispering all the while, they occasionally exchanged furtive glances with George and P.H. When the job was complete, they primped, combing one another's hair, and admiring their reflections in the window panes.

IT WAS POLLY who first noticed the snow. She was turning her head from side to side, studying herself from every possible angle when the first few flakes began drifting earthward. They were plump and airy and descended lazily as if in no hurry to land. "Snowing . . ." she said softly and with some uncertainty, as if she wasn't quite sure of what she'd seen. She studied the sky, oblivious now to her appearance. More snow. This time she spoke with confidence, "Snowing. Look, it's snowing."

Abruptly, the room hushed. There was a pause and then a unified gasp as we stampeded to the windows and watched. We held our breath. Could it be? Could anything so wonderful be happening to us? Nothing could have made the day better than snow—beautiful white snow—just before Christmas. And it *was* true! There they were— downy crystals, slowly pirouetting to the earth.

"It *is* snowing!" I shouted, and the room was instantly filled with double the sound and move-

Nothing could have made the day better than snow . . .

ment of the moments before the sighting. We jumped up and down, clapped our hands, and pressed our faces to the windows. Without asking permission, a few of us bolted to the door, threw it open, and ran into the wintry day. We held our arms out, turning palms and faces to the sky. We twirled and laughed until the cold drove us back to the shelter of school.

Within minutes, the snow was falling heavily, dusting the ground like sifted flour. Some settled down, but most of us remained at the windows, peacefully watching the snow's graceful descent. It looked like cottonwood shedding feathery seeds, except it was falling over a backdrop of dark gray rather than the faded blue of summer.

8

The Wind Comes

A WIND FROM THE NORTH soon joined the snow. Twisting and turning in the air, came more snowflakes, quicker now, their dainty sashay ended. Before long the ground was entirely covered in white. This was no flour dusting, this was a blanketing.

Some of the children left the windows and gathered near the piano. It was close enough to the wood stove to make it the warmest part of the room as well as the best lit. Mrs. Talley played quietly. Some sang along while others finished whatever preparations they were making for the pageant. I stayed by the window, too hypnotized by the spectacle to break away.

The timbre of the room changed following the sudden jubilation brought about by the snow. The peacefulness was palpable. Those of us at the windows talked quietly among ourselves in between long periods of silence.

Mary and P.H. sat with George and Polly who conversed in low tones and divided their time gazing wistfully at one another and then wistfully at the snow outside the window. The cold gave them reason to move not closer to the fire, but to each other. The glowing pot-bellied stove partially blocked them from Mrs. Talley's view. Mrs. Talley, however, missed nothing. She periodically leaned forward to keep an eye on them, all the while playing and singing along with the children gathered around her.

The snow fell steadily for about an hour when someone asked, "Mrs. Talley, what time is it?" She looked at her pocket watch. Her voice broke ranks with the meditative tone that had been set in our room. "Oh! It's two o'clock. I had no idea," she answered with some surprise. She stood up and took a step away from the piano. "Only half an hour before the show. Guests will be arriving. They'll be here any minute now." Mrs. Talley seemed unusually flustered. "Ready, everyone?"

"Yes, Mrs. Talley," responded twelve voices. She took in a long, deep breath and slowly exhaled. "Alright then, I do think we're ready. Now remember, boys, escort the ladies to their seats. Helen, Roma? Take their hats and coats. Quinn, Danny, take any dishes they bring and arrange them on the table. Oh, yes, everyone— remember your manners." She stopped and shook her head. "I don't know why I said that. You *always* remember your manners. You must be the most mannerly children in Texas, and the smartest." To this day, I believe she meant it.

Mrs. Talley played quietly . . .

With the exception of the lovesick Polly and George, all of us stood sentry near the windows, watching for the guests who were to arrive any minute.

9

The Blizzard

THE WIND picked up speed. At first, it had skimmed over the school yard like a mother's whispered shushing to soothe her crying baby. In swift increments, whispering rose to a low growl, which quickly turned to a tortured howling. Now the wind was vengeful, dashing snow to the ground. Drifts took shape as it blew snow hard against trees, boulders, and everything else in its path. Gathering momentum, it turned shrill, screeching its way through cracks in the schoolhouse walls, whipping the snow until the sky was obscured and all that could be seen was white—a fierce and frenzied dance of white.

"I'm cold," said Helen to no one in particular.

Mrs. Talley brought Helen's threadbare jacket to her and put it over her shoulders. "Here, Helen," she said, staying close while her eyes scanned the world outside. Even though there seemed to be plenty of wood stacked by the door, she must have felt we needed more. "George, would you bring in a few more logs? We may need them."

George, who had been sitting as close to Polly as he felt he legitimately could get away with, answered, "You bet, Mrs. Talley. I'm the man for the job." He winked at Polly and headed for the door.

"George," scolded Polly, "you wear a coat, hear?"

"I don't need any coat."

"George, you are to wear a coat," Mrs. Talley instructed. "Put it on." Her voice was unusually firm.

"Okay—uh, I mean, yes, Ma'am." George took his coat from one of the hooks next to the door. Slipping it on he announced, "All right, everybody, I'm going out. Send the cavalry if I'm not back in an hour." He smiled at Polly, "and make sure they wear *their* coats." Despite the fact that his joke was not especially funny, everyone was laughing as he pulled open the door. I had to admit, there was a charm about George.

A chilling blast of air hit the room. The cold, dry snow that had been forced against the door spilled into our school. Papers were whipped into the air. Some of the children shrieked in surprise and fear. All of us were alarmed. George paused for an instant and then hurriedly stepped outside, pulling the door shut behind him.

"I'd better help," P.H. said. He took his coat from the rack.

"Yes, P.H., you'd better," Mrs. Talley replied soberly.

A chilling blast of air hit the room.

P.H. opened the door cautiously, slipping out before more cold blasted through. Mrs. Talley looked down and sighed. I saw that my sister was crying.

"Roma, don't cry," I whispered to her.

"It's c-c-cold," she said between sobs, "and I want Daddy."

I didn't know what to say. I wanted my daddy, too.

"I think we should put on our coats. That will help us stay warm," Mrs. Talley suggested. She didn't need to ask twice. We took our coats down from their hooks and bundled ourselves in them as tightly as we could.

P.H. and George returned with armfuls of firewood. They stoked the fire and stacked what was left over next to the door. Mrs. Talley asked for our attention. "Children, let's gather over here, by the fire."

We went to her and waited.

"Sometimes, things happen that you just don't expect," she said. "We didn't expect this storm, did we?" She paused and watched us silently shake our heads. "And here we've been working *so hard* to be ready for our pageant. I am so proud of you. How I wish your families were able to come here today and . . ."

"Won't nobody be coming then?" someone called out.

"Anybody. Won't *anybody* be coming. . . ." she caught herself, "Oh, I'm sorry, now's not the time to worry about words." She cleared her throat. "No, I don't think anyone will be coming. I doubt that anyone could get through this storm. You couldn't see your hand in front of your face if you were out in it, and Mr. Turner's car would never make it."

"That's the truth," agreed P.H., "I couldn't hardly see nothin'—I mean anything—when I was out there."

"But my Mama will worry about me. She'll worry and worry and wonder when she'll see me again." Helen said.

"Helen, these storms don't last forever. Your mama knows that. All of your mothers and fathers know that. And they know we have lots of fire-wood, so we'll be warm. We'll even have plenty to eat. I brought some special treats for all of us—popcorn balls." She stopped for the sign of cheer that she hoped the promise of popcorn balls would bring. A few weak smiles were the only result. "Even if we have to spend the night, we'll be just fine." There wasn't much more to be said.

I went to the windows and leaned against a sill, cold as it was. Helen and Roma followed me. Roma wasn't crying anymore, but her eyes were red.

"This was Christmas," Helen stated flatly.

"It's not Christmas," I said. "Christmas won't be here for a week."

"But it was *our* Christmas," Helen said. "My mama's and mine. The pageant was my present to her, and the cookies she was bringing were her present to me. This is the only Christmas we get this year."

I thought about what she said. It never occurred to me until that moment that this was our Christmas, too. Roma and I knew there was no money for presents. Dinner would be no different than other dinners—red beans, maybe, and some carrots and potatoes we harvested before the cold set in. Of course there'd be biscuits. We'd become so tired of biscuits, even with wild plum jam.

"Last year, Momma and Daddy got us dolls from Sears and Roebucks," Roma said. "They ordered them from the catalog, and then Daddy made them chairs."

Jimmy wandered over in time to hear Roma's comment. "Maybe this year your daddy will make them a table."

Roma murmured, "Maybe." She and I both knew that Daddy worked nearly every moment he was awake. So did our mother. Any stick of wood that might become doll furniture went into the stove to keep us warm and to cook our food. I looked around. There was not a soul in the room that had much more than a roof over their head. Few of us could say for certain they had enough food to take them through the winter. We were lucky to eat—lucky to have any shelter, a warm school, and friends.

What we didn't know was that in the years to

come, we would live through far greater hardships—unfathomable hardships. Days upon days
of hunger, days upon days with the sun eclipsed by
thunderheads of dust, and loss—loss of loved
ones, homes, our way of life, and our childhoods.

10

Prints on the Window

O N T H E D A Y of the pageant, no one knew
what the next few years would bring. We
knew only that the glorious moment we
anticipated had been stolen from us. We were as
low in spirits as we could be and just plain sorry
for ourselves—sorry, cold, and afraid. Everyone
that is, except for Polly and George. They had
tossed caution to the wind and were holding
hands. It wouldn't have surprised me if they snuck
in a kiss or two when no one was watching.

P.H. and Mary had been edging closer to one
another, emboldened by the example set by Polly
and George. Quite likely, at least four of us were
delighted with the unexpected turn of events.

Jimmy spread his fingers wide and pressed
his hand on the window. "Cold," he said. "The
window's real cold. Touch it." Because there was
no longer hope for romance between Jimmy and
me, I felt comfortable going to him and placing
my hand next to his on the window. The window
was cold. I pulled my hand away. "Look," Jimmy

said, "see where your hand was." A ghost-like print of my hand remained on the glass.

I put my hand on the window again to make another print. Jimmy did the same. "My Dad shot a big rattler last summer," he said. "He gave me the rattle. Biggest rattle I every seen. I let Bill borrow it one day. He was supposed to give it back to me, but he lost it."

"My Dad killed a big rattler too, but he gave Roma the rattle 'cuz she was the oldest. I'll get the next one, prob'bly."

He took his hand off the glass and held it to his face. I did the same. "Cold, huh?" he said.

"Look at our prints," I said. We looked at them and then through them, into the blizzard.

"If I had that rattle—if Bill didn't go and lose it—I'd probably give it to you, if you wanted it," Jimmy said.

I must have blushed, because my face felt hot and tingly. I didn't know what to say, so I said nothing. We stood at the window, our eyes focused on the strange world outside the school. Neither of us was brave enough to look at the other at that moment.

A ghost-like print of my hand . . .

II

The Stranger in the Storm

SOMETHING OUTSIDE captured Jimmy's attention. "What's that?" he pointed toward the cottonwood grove that was across the field. I looked, but saw only the suggestion of trees through the white. "What?" I asked, straining to see whatever it was. "I don't see anything."

"Look, look real close. When the wind blows just so, you can see the big tree, the one next to the pond. There's something moving near it."

I peered into the blizzard, looking for something, anything. And there *was* something. Its form was vague and shadowy. At first it seemed as if my eyes were tricking me into seeing something that wasn't there, but I saw it—I saw it and watched as it moved toward us. It was too far away and too obscured by snow flurries to be identified as man or beast, but without question, it was there, and it was moving slowly, haltingly in our direction. "What is it?" I asked.

"Don't know; I think someone's coming." Jimmy called out to his brother, "P.H., what do you reckon that is?"

Heads popped up around the room and looked in the direction Jimmy was pointing. P.H. walked over. Others, curious and looking for a distraction, followed him. Even Polly and George abruptly dropped one another's hand and stood up. "What, Jimmy?" asked P.H.

"That, over there."

P.H. looked through the window, squinting. "Somethin'—it's somethin' alright. Somebody, more like it."

Mrs. Talley stood behind us. "It's definitely someone," she said, "but who could be out in this weather?" Within moments, everyone could see that the form in the snow was indeed a person, someone bundled up in a dark coat and approaching the school.

George and Polly walked over to where the rest of us were standing. Polly asked, "Do you think it's someone lost in the storm and needs help?"

"Yes, Polly, it could be, but I don't know. . . ." Mrs. Talley began. "He's certainly coming this way."

"Should I go out and help him?" George asked.

"Not just yet. . . . Let me think," Mrs. Talley answered. She held her chin with her hand and scrutinized the figure that was slowly but steadily trudging through the snow. It became evident that the figure wasn't a man, but a woman! She held a cane in one hand and a package in the other. Her head was covered by a dark scarf tied securely under her chin. Loose strands of silvery hair

Someone bundled up in a dark coat . . .

wisped about her face. She looked down each time she planted her cane in the snow. With every other step, she lifted her head and fixed her eyes on the school. Her movements, slow and cautious, had a rhythm to them; the planted cane, the lowered head, the step forward, the head lifted, and her eyes fixing on our school.

"I think . . . I think I may know who it is," said Mrs. Talley. "P.H., George!" The boys looked up. "Put on your coats. Our guest may need some help." P.H. and George scrambled into their coats and bolted for the door. Before opening it to charge into the blizzard, each caught the eye of his respective love interest. This assignment was frosting on their cakes. Not only had they saved the day by bringing in firewood, now they were about to rescue some stranded soul from the storm. Exuding bravado, the boys dashed through the door.

The misery that had descended on our classroom vanished. Excitement—it would not be an exaggeration to say, *exhilaration*—replaced it.

"Who is it?" we asked. "Who's coming?"

"I'm not entirely certain, but I think I know. . . ."

We watched P.H. and George struggle through the snow. The woman saw them and stopped, possibly thankful for a reason to rest. The boys reached her. We could see them conversing. Then P.H. took something from her hands, and George held out his arm for her. Together, they trudged back to the school.

"Let's all line up at the door to greet her when she arrives. Mary, take her package; Polly, her shawl and coat—that is unless she wants to keep them on. She'll be cold I imagine."

We scurried to line up at the door. Helen and I began to giggle and some others joined us. I don't know why. One lonely woman was plodding up to our door, and we were elated.

"Shush now," said Mrs. Talley. "She'll be here any minute."

12

Frenchie

THE SCHOOLHOUSE door opened. George and P.H. stood at the threshold, allowing the mystery guest and the furious wind to enter first. The boys forced the door to close, but all eyes were on the woman standing beside them.

When she first stepped into the room, she was looking down, having just placed her cane on the step to make sure of her footing. She was small and bent. Her nose and cheeks were rosy from the cold and looked out of place in her pale white face, crisscrossed and crevassed with wrinkles. Her coat and shawl were the darkest gray, nearly black. The coat must have been dinner to many a moth, as it was freckled with small, irregular holes. Threadbare elbows signified years of wear. With her white forehead and silver strands of hair sticking out from under the dark shawl, her form hidden in the long dark coat, she was a study in black and white. At first glance, she looked exactly like an illustration from a storybook to me—she was the witch that nearly tricked Hansel and Gretel into being her dinner.

And then she lifted her head.

What we saw were eyes the color of the sky in deepest summer, just after sunset when the moon is new. They were lit by a sparkle that must have been glowing somewhere within her, too strong and warm to be contained in her frail body. Suddenly, she was nothing like a witch.

"I'm sorry to be late," she said with the slightest French accent merged with a Texas drawl. "There's a bit of snow out, and I don't walk as fast as I once did."

"No, no, you're just in time, and we are so happy that you've come," replied Mrs. Talley. "Mrs. McCormick, let me introduce you to our class."

Mrs. McCormick, I thought. *This is Frenchie McCormick!* Mother had told me about her. Mother called her the "belle of the ball," whatever that meant. Father chuckled when Mother called her that. "Belle of something," he smirked, as if there was something funny about her that shouldn't be mentioned around children. Some of the children thought they knew about Frenchie. Their parents had given them only the sketchiest information, so the stories were fantastic accounts of her alignments with outlaws, gamblers, and women we weren't supposed to know about. And now, she was standing right in front of us. Mouths dropped open. We were struck dumb. As far as we were concerned, Christmas had come early to Tascosa.

"I brought some little cakes for you," she said, motioning to the package P.H. was holding.

"Thank you so much, Mrs. McCormick. Polly, please take our guest's coat and shawl." Polly, hearing her name, jerked out of the trance affecting all of us. She, too, was mesmerized by the presence of the mystery woman. Polly followed Mrs. Talley's directions, reverently taking Frenchie's things and curtsying slightly as she turned to put the coat away.

If Frenchie had taken any pains to dress herself that day, it wasn't obvious. She was still wearing the apron she had apparently worn for baking. Her dress was plain and gray. Who would have known she once dressed in satin, velvet, and lace? Her hair was up in a bun, but not an especially successful one. We took it all in—the misplaced locks of hair hanging indiscriminately over her shoulders, the way she tried to gather and pin them into the bun once her shawl was removed, and the shrug as she gave up and turned her attention to us.

"Mrs. McCormick, this is such an honor. Children, our show must be especially good. Mrs. McCormick was once on the stage herself. She was a famous performer, and now we will perform for her. Mrs. McCormick, please, have a seat, here in the front row."

"But, where are the others? You mustn't start without the rest of your audience."

"Frenchie . . . I mean, Mrs. McCormick, you are the only one who made it here. The storm was too much for everyone else. But, we're rested and rehearsed, and you know as well as we do, the show must go on."

THE SHOW did go on. I wish I could remember all of the songs we sang, all the poems and our skit, but all I remember was my big moment when I sang "Up on the Rooftop." Mrs. Talley accompanied me on the piano, and I belted out the song, remembering her instructions—"enunciate each word, keep in time with the music, and remember to smile at the audience."

I smiled at the audience, and the audience smiled back at me, with eyes bright as footlights. I kept time with the music and she, too, kept time, gently tapping her foot with the beat. I thought I saw her lips moving as if she wanted to sing along. My heart was full. There was no sadness or disappointment within me. This day, indeed, was like no other. The pageant was a success. Beautiful snow dressed the earth. Jimmy liked me. I liked Jimmy. And I sang for the Belle of Old Tascosa.

And I sang for the Belle of Old Tascosa.

May 2, 2005 —An Epilogue

THAT WAS THE STORY our mother told us that Thanksgiving morning. I have just spent the last three days on the Texas Panhandle with my mother and my sister Susan, visiting the places where Mother had lived so many years ago. The site where Tascosa used to be is now Cal Farley's Boys Ranch, a home for children who might otherwise not have a home. All that remains from Mother's days are the courthouse, Boot Hill, and the schoolhouse where twelve children gathered with Mrs. Talley at the piano and put on the most amazing Christmas pageant.

I was wearing sandals and a light cotton skirt as I rushed from my hotel this morning and found myself in a rare and record snow fall—in May, no less, in the desert Southwest. Yet to my astonishment, there it was—five inches and more falling. To find my rental car, I pointed and clicked my electronic key at each of the white mounds in the parking lot until I heard a muffled honk. Then, when it was not quite daylight, I cautiously drove to the Amarillo airport to catch a flight back to Seattle. As I write this, I'm sitting on the tarmac waiting for the wings of the jet to be de-iced. My laptop is on the tray table. I probably have another half hour to write before it's safe to fly, and I'll need to put it away. I'm trying to decide how this story should end.

If it were only about Tascosa, Frenchie, and the Christmas pageant, then I suppose the story should end when Frenchie clapped, and the girls curtseyed and the boys bowed and, somehow, once the storm abated, everyone made it home. There could be a footnote or two about Frenchie's funeral, which was a decade later, complete with six residents from Cal Farley's Boys Ranch singing, "Home on the Range" as her casket was lowered into the ground next to Mickey's. I could end it by telling about Cal Farley, the visionary who created the Boy's Ranch, a truly remarkable home for children. But this story is about something more. I think it is about a gift.

Frenchie, with her hair pulled up haphazardly into a bun, in her dark woolen, moth-eaten, and frayed dress, and with her sapphire eyes twinkling out from her wrinkled face, brought twelve children that gift. She brought it from New Orleans, cloaked in mystery. She filled it with exuberance, color, and gaiety as she danced, smiling and laughing across the stage. Her gift was sanctified by her enduring love for Mickey; and Mickey gave it faith by loving her in return. Tested by the dust storms, hunger, and despair of the Great Depression, the gift held patiently as Frenchie waited for Tascosa to rise again.

On that snowy day in December 1931, Frenchie carried the gift through a storm that others dared not brave. Trudging through deep white powder with little between her and the cold, she delivered the gift to twelve children who had given up hope, just when they were on the brink of a time when only hope could sustain them. That was Frenchie's gift, of course: hope.

I wonder if, in any way, Frenchie's gift helped my mother bear the agonizing years that followed. Through those years, she became a beautiful, strong, and ferociously brave woman, and later, a beloved teacher, mother, and grandmother. In any event, she didn't squander the gift. She nurtured it so it would grow and even passed it on to many others, including me. I suspect that hope must be shared to grow. So the end of this story is now up to you.

AFTERWORD

Quintille Speck-Firman Garmany

OVER SEVENTY Christmases have come and gone since that Christmas in Old Tascosa. I live on another panhandle now, in Florida. The time that stands between today and 1931 has absorbed countless memories, but the memory of that Christmas, the one when I met Frenchie, has survived. So have other memories of those days.

By the Christmas of 1932, my family had left Tascosa and few of my classmates would remain long. No jobs were to be found there, and when the dust showered down on us and the heavens withheld the rain, crops no longer grew. Polly's family left for California, along with many others. I understand that Mrs. Talley didn't teach at the school the next year. How I hope she continued to teach somewhere so other children could have the honor of learning from her, learning so much more than reading and mathematics. The Balfours stayed for a few more years, even though their ranch had become worthless. Mrs. Balfour wrote a few times before we lost track of their family. I was glad when she stopped writing; her letters brought little but sadness. One of them had news about Jimmy. His appendix burst in 1932, and his parents couldn't get him to a hospital; he died on his way to Amarillo, maybe in Mr. Turner's car, I don't know.

My family left when the gravel pit shut down. We moved to Canyon, Texas, into a house with gaping holes where the door and windows should have been. My father scavenged scraps of wood to cover the empty spaces. He never saw the ineffectiveness of those makeshift coverings. Father, whose love I never doubted and still do not doubt, left to find work and then followed in the footsteps of Helen's father. He never came back. He never saw how the dust swept through Texas, coating our world in powdery gray. He wasn't there when our house burned to the ground, and we were forced to live in an even smaller shack, kindly offered to us by townspeople who had the heart and the wherewithal to help. He wasn't there to watch when Mother took our baby brother and left to find work in Amarillo, leaving Jane, Roma, and me behind to care for one another. He never knew.

Now that I've told this story, it seems like fantasy. Could we have been so poor, have had so little? Could life have been so bleak? The truthful answer is "yes," but that truth does not veil another, greater truth. Amidst the hardships, I found deep, enduring joy—in the songs of the meadowlarks, in the clear night skies of summer—and yes, in Texas northers whose furies

Old Tascosa Schoolhouse, 1991

sometimes left the prairie carpeted in snow. I learned and played with other children, who, like me, found more joy in a simple Christmas pageant than in anything that could be placed beneath a tree.

The hard days of the Dust Bowl cannot be overstated, and I won't pretend that my family lived through them without suffering. But when I went back to Tascosa with my daughters, so many years later, I could recall, but not *feel* any of the hardships I knew then. What I could—and did—feel was the happiness and the optimism that I knew as a child in Tascosa.

IF YOU WERE TO VISIT the Old Tascosa School, you would see the stump of a once stately tree resting on its grounds. When I was seven, I played beneath that tree. Jimmy and I ran circles around it, chasing one another, oblivious to everything but the delight of the moment. George carved his name into it, next to Polly's. Helen and I sat in its shade, trading secrets and dreaming about what we'd do when we were grown up.

A pot-bellied stove and a piano still furnish the school's interior. When I returned to Tascosa and stood in that room again, I saw Mrs. Talley once more, through the lens of memory. She was sitting at the piano and saying, "Children, what shall we sing this morning?" I saw my classmates assembled around her, still flushed from the morning race. Some of them were raggedy, some of them neat as pins, a few were fidgeting, and others composed. Most were hungry. But each glowed with anticipation of what the day might bring. I saw myself, eyes wide and fingers crossed, hoping that the morning's song would be "The Red River Valley."

I would trade nothing for those days, not their innocent pleasures or their struggles through which my strength was tempered. Recalling them, I believe that like Frenchie, I, too, could forge my way through a blizzard.

FRENCHIE MCCORMICK

Red Steagall and Richard O'Brien

The last time I saw her
She's standin' alone
In the door of her tumbledown shack
On the edge of Tascosa,
She's waited for years
But Mickey, her love, can't come back.

Mickey had died
Back in 19 and 12
But Frenchie had made him a vow
She'd stay in Tascosa
As long as she lived
It was tough, but she made it somehow.

CHORUS

Frenchie McCormick was true to her word.
She never left Mickey alone.
She stayed in that rotten, old tumbledown shack
By the edge of the Tascosa Road.
And the northern winds blew 'cross the
    Panhandle Plains
The winters were bitter and cold.

Frenchie McCormick, probably 1939

But she wouldn't move, was determined to
    keep
A promise she made long ago.

She came to Tascosa
From somewhere back East
A charming and pretty young lass.
She called herself Frenchie
But that's all we know
Because she never spoke of her past.

Mickey, a barkeep
A handsome young lad
Was as dashing a man as you'd find.
He hired the young beauty
They soon fell in love
And were married in just a short time.

CHORUS

She visited Mickey
Most every day
We'll come back without her this time
In a solemn procession
We trudge up the hill,
Six boys and a coffin of pine.

Yes, she kept her promise
She stayed 'till she died.
The stuff that romance is made of.
On a small windblown hill
Overlooking the town
She lays beside Mickey, her love.

CHORUS

ACKNOWLEDGMENTS

M Y SIBLINGS and I were raised on stories about our mother's early life on the Texas panhandle, but for some reason, the story of the 1931 Old Tascosa Christmas pageant was withheld from us until we were all quite grown and of the opinion that Mother had exhausted her cache of childhood anecdotes. How happy we were to be wrong. On Thanksgiving Day, 2004, she recounted the story that is the subject of this book. I have tried to remain faithful to the facts, as she remembered them. However, memories spanning over seven decades can, and will, have flaws.

Over the months spent finalizing this book, I frequently consulted with Mother, checking and rechecking facts. "What did you wear? What did you eat? What sort of car did Mr. Turner drive? What songs did Mrs. Talley play on the piano? What was the object of the game, Annie Over?" Even minds as sharp as my mother's can become clouded, especially when overtaxed. At one point she began questioning the year in which the pageant took place. Maybe it was in 1932, not 1931—or perhaps 1933. She first recalled that Mr. Turner drove a Model A, but later determined it was a Desoto, and the following week she thought it may have been a LaSalle.

The National Weather Service provided us with data to establish that the pageant most likely took place on December 16, 1931, Mother's first memory being the correct one. We are still uncertain about Mr. Turner's car, but it was big enough to transport five and sometimes seven children; quite likely a Desoto, but that remains unconfirmed. I needed to create names for a few of the classmates whose names had been forgotten, and of course, I crafted the dialogue. What the students actually said and did that day can not be written without the benefit of a time machine, so I wrote the parts that Mother felt certain about and borrowed from her accounts of other school days to fill in the blanks. In other words, these things happened, but not necessarily on the day of the pageant. But for those exceptions, the story is faithful to the events of December 16, 1931, in Old Tascosa.

This story would never have been written had not my sister, Susan Quinn Goodwin, insisted that Mother tell it. It might never have been published had my brother, Rebb Firman, not taken it upon himself to e-mail the manuscript to Red Steagall, who in turn sent it to Judith Keeling at Texas Tech University Press. I thank them all.

I owe a huge debt of gratitude to my cousin and friend, Wendy Firman Isenhart, who read draft after draft and offered many on target editing suggestions. Thanks also to the following friends who helped me in various and sundry ways as I put the story together: Susan Janko Summers, Margaret Lord, Jane Newton-McCoy, Holly Mc-Donald Johnson, Barbara Wade, Mary Margaret Cromanty, and Kathy Gustin. Brian Fisher deserves more than a little credit for his role in facilitating our fact-finding trip to the Texas Panhandle, and for his ongoing love and support. I offer a special thanks to Cathy Lexa and Sherm and Genie Harriman, without their help, Mother would never have had the opportunity to step back inside the Old Tascosa Schoolhouse, which still stands, on the grounds of the Cal Farley Boys' Ranch.

Finally, I want to thank my mother and co-author, Quintille Firman-Garmany. Susan, Rebb, and I are fortunate to have such a remarkable woman for a mother. And with it, I pass along the hope she gave to me—given with profound love and reciprocated with my deep admiration.

PHOTO CREDITS

Photos on pages 81 and 84 are courtesy of the Julian Bivins Museum, Cal Farley's Boys' Ranch.